Tracks *in* Time
A Children's History of Estes Park

Patricia P. Pickering
Patricia Y. Washburn

Illustrated by
Patricia H. Greenberg

One day while speaking to Brooke Fortini, a third grade teacher in Estes Park, I found out that though local history is taught, no children's books on the subject are available to the classes. I began talking to people interested in elementary education, and with the encouragement of the Board of the Friends & Foundation Inc. of the Estes Park Museum, I decided to attempt to fill that void. You might call it serendipity that Pat Greenberg works as a volunteer at the Museum and her time slot is right after mine so, through the years, we have gotten to know each other. With the book in mind, I asked her if she would be interested in this project and she agreed to work on the illustrations. Pat Washburn, a Friends & Foundation Board member, thought she could be helpful with the writing and the history, so she came on board as well. And thus began the saga of "the three Pats," as everyone referred to us!

I am very grateful to all those who have contributed to the success of *Tracks in Time*. Pat Greenberg's artistic talents helped to create a book that is both delightful and unique. Pat Washburn willingly allowed us to take advantage of her wealth of historical knowledge and contributed to the text. Alicia Mittelman, Curator of Education and Collections at the Estes Park Museum, met with us, read and helped edit the texts, located photographs, and lent her support during our many iterations of the book. Derek Fortini, Estes Park Museum Manager and Curator of Exhibits, was always available - helpful, encouraging, and the voice of reason. Nancy Thomas, the editor of the Friends & Foundation Press, shepherded us through the process of bringing a book to print. My husband, Jim, read and edited the text and his great enthusiasm for this project was a constant encouragement.

Pat Pickering

The history of early Estes Park is a collection of stories of individuals - self-reliant, hard working men and women who came to the valley to visit and then stayed to establish homes and businesses. Native Americans were the first to come, but they were followed by many others: hunters, homesteaders, geologists, prospectors, mountaineers, government workers, artists, writers and vacationers. It is their accomplishments, successes and failures that provided the foundation of the town's early character and history. These pioneer settlers started it all! Follow the bobcat as he leads you through our history.

I just thought I'd wait a minute for you to catch up with me. We'll be heading down this path towards the town of Estes Park. Along the way we'll see many beautiful sights and meet many interesting folks. I've asked my friends, the Twin Owls, to join us.
They may have a question or two to ask you!

RACCOON

MARMOT

PIKA

BEAR

Wherever you are in Estes Park, there is wonderful scenery. Some small mountains are close to town. In the 1920s Old Man Mountain was a site for ski competitions, and the ski run is still visible from Fall River Road. Prospect Mountain has a tram running up its side. Lumpy Ridge, with MacGregor Ranch at its base, is a well-known rock climbing area and has a distinct formation called the Twin Owls. Larger mountains are located within the boundaries of Rocky Mountain National Park. Longs Peak is the highest mountain in the National Park and looks like it has a large beaver climbing up its side. Ypsilon Mountain has a "Y" shaped crevice, and Mummy Mountain looks like an Egyptian mummy.

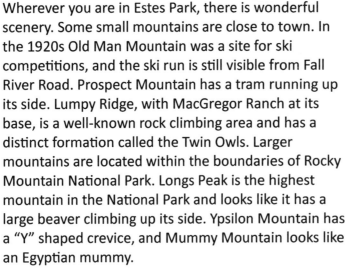

The Estes Park area provides outstanding viewing of wildlife. People come from all over the country to see the animals and birds "up close and personal." Elk and mule deer are seen in the largest numbers and hardly a day passes without spotting some around town. In the fall, bull elk bugle to attract females. The mating season is called "the rut" and is so popular that the Town has a festival devoted to celebrating this annual event. Bighorn sheep also rut in the fall. Some animals, such as ptarmigan and hares, change their color to white to hide in the winter snow.

ELK

HAGUES

MUMMY

FAIRCHILD

YPSILON

CHIQUITA

CHAPIN

BIGHORN

TURKEY

LUMPY RIDGE

CASTLE

DEER

RMNP 34

RMNP

OLD MAN

OLYMPUS 34

36

PROSPECT

36

7

GIANT TRACK

COYOTE

RAMSHORN

LILY

WHICH ANIMALS ARE FOUND IN THE VALLEY AND WHICH LIVE IN THE HIGH COUNTRY?

FLATTOP

HALLETT

OTIS

ESTES CONE

TWIN SISTERS

THATCHTOP

STORM

LADY WASHINGTON

TAYLOR

POWELL

McHENRYS

LONGS PEAK

CHIEFS HEAD

PAGODA

MEEKER

N

W — E

S

SNOWSHOE HARE

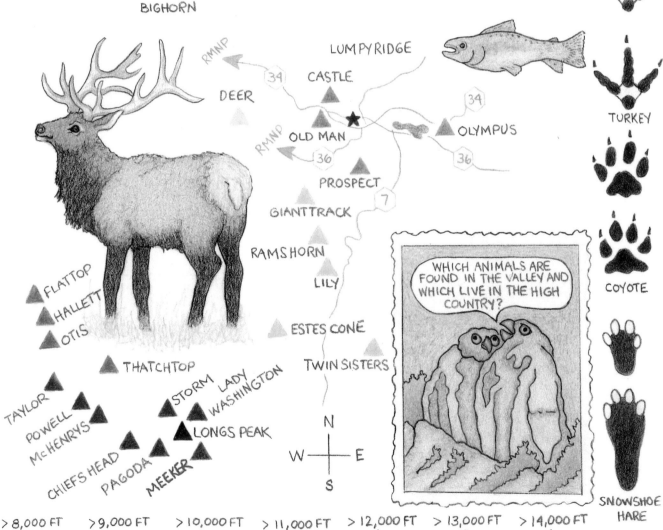

> 8,000 FT   > 9,000 FT   > 10,000 FT   > 11,000 FT   > 12,000 FT   > 13,000 FT   > 14,000 FT

High up on the tundra of Rocky Mountain
National Park there are remains
of low rock walls used for game drives.
Warriors hid behind them
when hunting large animals.
There is also evidence of teepee rings
in favorite camping areas.

Arapaho expedition

Arapaho elders Sherman Sage and Gun Griswald returned to Estes Park in 1914 to accompany Oliver Toll and Shep Husted on a pack trip. Their purpose was to point out sites and trails and to recall the original names of places. Tom Crispin, who was part Arapaho, translated for the group. Toll's record of the expedition was published as *Arapaho Names and Places*.

The Native Americans knew the Estes Park area well. Following ancient trails, the Ute came for spring hunting about 900 years ago. In 1780-1800, the Arapaho and their allies the Cheyenne, moved into the mountains. This caused a short period of war over hunting grounds. Native Americans made Estes Park their summer home, and some of their trails became our modern roads. Arrowheads and stone implements have been found throughout the valley. By 1859, when Joel Estes arrived, the Native Americans had already relocated to other areas.

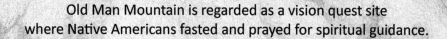

Old Man Mountain is regarded as a vision quest site where Native Americans fasted and prayed for spiritual guidance.

A Ute "wikiup" served as temporary shelter

Joel Estes and his son Milton discovered the valley during the fall of 1859. He returned the following summer and built two log homes and several corrals in the area below the present high school. The site is now under Lake Estes. From 1863–1866 Joel, Milton, and their families lived there. The summers were wonderful, but the winters were long, harsh and lonely. Joel hunted elk, moose, deer, sheep and bear. Fish were also plentiful and fresh milk available from the dairy cows they kept. The first winter was somewhat mild, but the winter of 1864 was very severe. This made the Estes family decide not to stay, so in April 1866 they sold their property and moved away.

Estes Memorial

Estes Park Hotel

Windham Thomas Wyndham-Quin, the Earl of Dunraven, arrived in Estes Park in 1872. He was involved in a huge land fraud scheme, illegally gathering 6,000 acres of valuable land along rivers, creeks and springs. While here, he built a lodge and a cottage, then a large hotel. He called it the "Estes Park Hotel," but it was known locally as the "English Hotel." It opened in 1877 and operated until August 1911, when it was destroyed by fire. The Earl traveled most of the year and only visited Estes Park two or three times. In June 1908 he sold his land to F. O. Stanley and a partner, ending his ties with Estes Park.

Griff Evans and his family arrived in the fall of 1867, moving into the cabins that the Estes family left. He was described as a small jovial man who supported his family by hunting and then selling the meat in Denver. Later he became more prosperous raising cattle. Finally the family built additional cabins in order to accommodate tourists who wanted to visit the beautiful valley and surrounding mountains.

Sprague's Lodge

Estes-Evans Ranch

In 1875, **Abner Sprague** built a homestead in Estes Park. He operated saw mills, was a surveyor and constructed and operated resorts. He also ran a stage line transporting visitors to Estes Park and Moraine Park [originally called "Willow Park"], and explored and named many of the places located in what would become Rocky Mountain National Park.

Isabella Lucy Bird, a free-spirited and adventuresome English woman, arrived in Estes Park in October, 1873. She stayed only a few months, but wrote about her experiences in letters to her sister in England. Later Bird edited the 17 letters and used them to create her famous book, *A Lady's Life in the Rocky Mountains*. During her stay she traveled 700 miles around central Colorado on her horse "Birdie."
In her letters she often mentions Rocky Mountain Jim. He helped her climb Longs Peak and they developed a deep friendship while Isabella lived here.

James Nugent, **"Rocky Mountain Jim,"** was a colorful character made famous by English writer Isabella Bird. Jim was a hunter, trapper, fisherman and mountaineer with a mysterious past. In 1871, while hunting, Jim was maimed by a bear. As a result of the fight, Jim lost his right eye. After recovering, he returned to his squatter's claim near Estes Park. In June 1874, during an argument, Griff Evans shot at Jim. Some buckshot ricocheted off a wagon wheel and hit Jim in the back of his head. He died in Fort Collins on September 7. He was buried there in an unmarked grave on September 12.

The Rocky Mountain News reported that Jim had 50 scars on his body. The bear bit through his left arm, ripped his scalp down to the bone, tore off his left thumb and mangled one side of his face.

F. O. Stanley

Stanley Hotel

Freelan Oscar [F.O.] Stanley and his wife Flora came to Estes Park in 1903. In 1908 he and a partner bought the Earl of Dunraven's lands. By June 1909 the beautiful three-story Stanley Hotel, overlooking the village, was finished. He built a summer home and a small hydroelectric plant on Fall River. He founded the Estes Park Bank and the Estes Park Transportation Company. Stanley helped establish the town's water and sewer system. He bought several lots on Elkhorn Avenue and put up a large garage and office. This became the transportation company for his steam cars and Mountain Wagons, which were used to pick up travelers from the Lyons and Loveland train stations. This building later became the Park Theatre Mall, which burned down in October 2009.

Historic Fall River Hydroplant

Stanley Steamers at the train depot in Lyons

MacGregor Ranch then and now

Muriel Lurilla MacGregor was the granddaughter of the pioneers Alexander and Clara MacGregor. Within Alex and Clara's lifetimes, MacGregor Ranch grew to 1200 acres on which they raised cattle and hosted tourists. Guests could either pitch tents on ranch property along Black Canyon Creek or rent a cabin. Muriel studied at the University of Denver and became a lawyer in 1936. She eventually returned home to Estes Park and took over responsibility for the ranch which had grown larger by that time. After her death, The MacGregor Trust gained ownership of the property and runs it as a working ranch and museum.

For many years Estes Park did not have an elected government. Three organizations played important roles in helping support the town and solving its civic problems: the Estes Park Protective and Improvement Association, the Estes Park Woman's Club, and the Estes Park Business Men's Association. In 1917 incorporation papers were filed to create the Town of Estes Park, which provided for an elected Board of Trustees with six members plus a mayor. This model continues today. The Woman's Club is the only one of the original three organizations to remain active.

The town of Estes Park now and then

ROCKY MOUNTA[IN] DEDICATION

Enos Mills

Enos Abijah Mills was a naturalist and owned Longs Peak Inn. At the age of 14 he came to stay with relatives in Estes Park and a year later started building a homestead cabin below Twin Sisters Mountain. In 1885 he made his first ascent of Longs Peak and eventually completed over 300 summits of the mountain. He became a popular lecturer for the Forest Service and wrote essays on nature and conservation subjects. Along with others, he initiated a campaign to establish a national park in the area. The official dedication of the National Park on September 4, 1915 marked a huge career achievement. He became known as the "Father of Rocky Mountain National Park."

Joe Mills

Enoch Josiah [Joe] Mills, the younger brother of Enos Mills, arrived in Estes Park in 1899. After attending Colorado Agricultural College in Fort Collins, he worked summers helping his brother manage the Longs Peak Inn. He excelled at collegiate sports, becoming a coach and athletic director at schools in Texas. In 1911, he returned to the Estes Park area to manage the Forks Hotel in Drake. In 1914, he built the Crags Hotel on Prospect Mountain. In 1918, he became the football coach and athletic director at the University of Colorado. He wrote short stories, essays and books with nature themes. Joe was involved with many of Estes Park's civic organizations, and was President of the Chamber of Commerce.

IN NAT'L PARK
SEP. 4. 1915

Beautiful **Rocky Mountain National Park** was not always a protected area. Over 100 years ago people began to worry that hunters, loggers, miners and ranchers would destroy the beauty of the area. Conservationists, including Enos Mills and F. O. Stanley, campaigned to protect these natural resources. They argued for the creation of a park that would forever be available for the public to enjoy. On January 26, 1915 President Wilson signed the bill establishing Rocky Mountain National Park.

Trail Ridge Road

One of the early Superintendents of Rocky Mountain National Park was **Roger Toll**. He served from 1921-1929 and oversaw construction of ranger stations, ranger housing, and the Park's equipment storage area. He also had a shelter cabin built on Longs Peak in memory of Agnes Vaille. Probably his most important work was to begin the construction of Trail Ridge Road, one of the most scenic national park highways in the United States. Today over three million people a year visit Rocky Mountain National Park and many of them drive this beautiful road. Roger Toll was the cousin of Oliver Toll, who led the Arapaho pack trip in 1914.

15

In 1874, William and Ella James built a homestead cabin near Lumpy Ridge. In 1877 they traded with another homesteader for land on Fall River just west of the future town of Estes Park. There they began raising cattle but soon discovered that the lodging of tourists was a more lucrative business. By 1881 they had a resort large enough to house 35–40 tourists; by 1885 the dining room in the lodge could serve 80 people. In 1890 "The Casino" was finished, providing additional recreational facilities. In the early 1900s a new and much larger **Elkhorn Lodge** was completed, with wings added later. The first school [about 1883] was held in one of the Elkhorn's original cottages. The school lasted two or three years and then was moved into a building in town.

LODGE & CAMP ACTIVITIES
DAILY HORSE RIDES
HIKING & CLIMBING
HUNTING
DANCES & PARTIES
CARD GAMES
LECTURES & MUSICALS
ONE-ARMED BANDIT
SWIMMING
TAFFY PULLS
HARVEST MOON PARTY
3 MEALS SERVED DAILY

Elkhorn Lodge

Community building

Rocky Mountain Boys Camp was established in 1919 on the hillside above Hallowell Park in Rocky Mountain National Park. The camp property contained a livery, baseball diamond, tennis courts, basketball court, and swimming pool. The campers went on long trips, such as a 500 mile, 6-day hiking and camping expedition to the Medicine Bow Mountains in Wyoming. The camp, among the very first in the Estes Park region, continued until 1951.

The Olinger Highlanders was founded in 1916 for boys 10-years-old and above. It was a type of military camp. All the boys came from Denver to an annual gathering based at Glacier Basin in Rocky Mountain National Park. It began with about 100 boys, but later grew to around 500-600. They wore military uniforms and practiced drills, frequently marching and giving demonstrations to the general public. The camp continued into the 1950s.

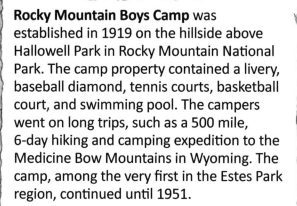

Frank Cheley developed the most successful summer youth camp in Estes Park history. **Cheley Camps** began at Bear Lake in 1921 with a camp for boys between the ages of 10-17. By 1926 a girls camp was added. A year later the camps were relocated to a larger area on the side of Twin Sisters Mountain. In 1937 additional property was purchased near the town of Glen Haven and became the site for two Trails End camps, concentrating on hiking and horseback riding.

In 1909 the YMCA purchased Wind River Lodge, including 344 acres and buildings, for a permanent summer camp. At first, most of the accommodations were sleeping tents. By 1918, almost all of these had been replaced with more substantial wooden housekeeping cottages and tent houses. The camp's reputation as a summer destination was then well established. The **YMCA of the Rockies Family Camp** has continued to expand through the years and now is a very large complex with a number of children's and teen day camps.

Accidents are to be expected when hiking and climbing in the mountains, but many times these turn into tragedies. Longs Peak stands out as the most dangerous mountain, although many other peaks have seen mishaps as well. Often fickle mountain weather is part of the problem. If you read or listen to the news, you will learn about several deaths occurring each year.

Agnes Vaille

Agnes Vaille was a very experienced hiker and mountain climber. On January 11, 1925, she made the first successful winter ascent of the East Face of Longs Peak. She was with another climber, Walter Kiener. They had made three previous attempts but each time had to turn back. This time they got a late start and had difficulty with snow and ice. They needed to cut ice steps up a steep incline and couldn't reach the summit until 4:00 a.m. Vaille was so exhausted from the climb that she didn't have the strength to make the return trip. When she tried to get over a large boulder, she fell and slid down a snowy slope. As daylight came, Kiener left her in a protected area and continued down to look for help. He finally found a rescue party, but it was too late. Vaille had frozen to death on the Boulder Field.

On October 16, 2010, **James Charles Patrick** was climbing Taylor Glacier with two companions when he fell more than 1,000 feet to his death. Patrick was carrying the rope used by all three, which left the other two stranded near the top of the glacier. They anchored themselves in place and then called for help using a cell phone. National Park rangers reached the ridgeline above the climbers after four hours and were able to help them to safety. Other rangers stayed with Patrick's body overnight until it was flown out the following morning.

Rescue helicopter

In August 1915, **Rev. Thornton Sampson** had been trekking in the mountains. He planned to cross Flattop Mountain, come down Odessa Gorge, and spend the night at Fern Lake. Then he was going to attend the Rocky Mountain National Park dedication. On September 3, when he started up Flattop, the weather was mild. Soon he encountered high winds and clouds. The trail became covered by heavy snow. Sampson never arrived at the ceremony. Search parties were sent out for weeks. Seventeen years later, a skeleton with a fractured left leg was found in Odessa Gorge. Nearby the minister's knapsack and diary were discovered. Rev. Sampson had been found.

Christiensen Memorial

Sometimes even National Park Service rangers have fatal accidents. On July 29, 2005, **Jeff Christiensen** was on backcountry patrol in the Mummy Range and fell to his death. His body was not found for several days because, after his accident, Jeff had been unable to use his radio to let people know his location. A memorial plaque and a sculpture of a ranger hat outside the Beaver Meadows Visitor Center of Rocky Mountain National Park commemorate Jeff Christiensen.

Dams on mountain lakes help furnish water to farms along the Front Range. The Grand Ditch was built to provide water for the Fort Collins area. But more water was needed. It was decided that a tunnel could be built under Rocky Mountain National Park from Grand Lake to Estes Park. Digging started from both east and west ends in June 1939, with the work moving towards the middle. The "holing through" of the tunnel occurred in June 1944. By then the workers had drilled through more than 13 miles of granite and the two tunnel holes matched almost perfectly. This impressive construction is called the **Colorado-Big Thompson Project**. In Estes Park, the biggest changes to be seen are the enlargement of Marys Lake, the new conduit pipes on the side of Prospect Mountain, the Marys Lake and Estes Park power plants, the creation of Lake Estes and the construction of Olympus Dam.

Estes valley then and now

Colorado-Big Thompson Project

A dam at Lawn Lake, in Rocky Mountain National Park, broke on the morning of July 15, 1982. It sent water racing down Roaring River into Endovalley and Horseshoe Park. The debris left behind formed a dramatic alluvial fan. Then the water surged towards town, dislodging everything in its path – boulders, trees, cars, buildings, propane tanks, trailer homes and bridges. It severely damaged the old hydroplant on Fall River, which had still been generating electricity. Once the water reached town, it rushed down Elkhorn Avenue, flooding the lower levels of many buildings. When the water joined the Big Thompson River, it swept on into Lake Estes, continuing the destruction. Fortunately, Olympus Dam was strong enough to hold back the water. Three people were killed in the **Lawn Lake Flood**.

Lawn Lake Flood

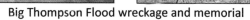

Big Thompson Flood wreckage and memorial

On July 31, 1976, a massive thunderstorm stalled over Estes Park. Pounding rain caused a wall of water to roar down the Big Thompson Canyon towards Loveland, with the river rising as high as 19 feet in some areas. It was the largest natural disaster in Colorado state history. The **Big Thompson Flood** demolished homes, businesses, parts of Highway 34 and killed 139 people. Along the road today are signs warning people to climb to higher ground when there is a chance of flooding. These signs were put in place in the hope that such loss of life will never happen again.

IN CASE OF FLOODING CLIMB TO HIGHER GROUND

Town Hall with fire trucks

Fires were a danger in early settlements. When a fire broke out in a store or home, everyone in the area came as quickly as possible to help put it out. In 1907, a volunteer fire department was organized. Through the years the department modernized its equipment. It also moved into its own building. Now the department is part of the **Estes Valley Fire District** and has a permanent Fire Chief.

The Birch Ruins are visible on top of the hill above the Estes Valley Public Library and the Municipal Building. Al Birch was a newspaper reporter for the *Denver Post*. He built his dream house high on the cliff with incredible views of the mountains. During construction a carpenter mistakenly ran the wooden floor joists under the fireplace. On a bitterly cold night in December 1907, the joists beneath the hearth caught fire, and the house burned. Its ruins can still be visited by means of a trail on top of the Knoll–Willows Open Space.

The Birch Ruins

Lewiston Hotel fire

The luxurious **Lewiston Hotel** was built on the west side of town and rivaled the Stanley Hotel. It had three stories, hot-and-cold running water, a third floor ballroom with an organ, and a roof-top garden. On September 4, 1941, a fire broke out in the attic and the building was completely destroyed. All that remains are the stone verandas of the hotel. These are now part of the foundations of townhouses built on the site.

Park Theatre Mall fire

Early on the morning of October 19, 2009, the historic **Park Theatre Mall** in the downtown business district was completely destroyed by fire. While the fire raged out of control, thick smoke filled the town. Fire fighters fought the flames from the outside because the Mall's metal roof was unstable. Though the Mall contained 12 separate businesses, there were no fire alarms or sprinkler systems. After several hours, the fire crews were able to take control of the flames. Most of the damage was confined to the mall shops and did not spread to adjoining buildings or the theater.

Estes Park

Celebrates

Independence Day, the **Fourth of July**, is celebrated with the "Coolest Car Show in Colorado" during the day and spectacular fireworks over Lake Estes at night. These events attract thousands of spectators every year.

Children do not go door-to-door on **Halloween** in Estes Park. Instead, Elkhorn Avenue becomes a pedestrian mall and the stores close early to prepare for costumed participants playing "Trick or Treat."

The **"Catch the Glow" Parade** is held on the Friday of Thanksgiving weekend and marks the beginning of the holiday season. A visit from Santa Claus is the finale of the event. The town is decorated for the holidays. Twinkling lights on the trees make it look like a winter wonderland.

The **Scottish-Irish Highland Festival** is held the weekend after Labor Day. The parade along Elkhorn Avenue is on Saturday morning, with marching bagpipe bands and clan members. During the four-day festival, the town is filled with participants wearing traditional tartans and kilts. Many are in the Highland Games or Pipe and Drum Band competitions.

The **Rodeo Parade** is held on the opening day of the Rooftop Rodeo in July. Most of the people in the parade represent groups that are interested in horses, such as dude ranches, resorts, camps, and liveries. Representatives come from other states and counties, like rodeo queens and their courts.

25

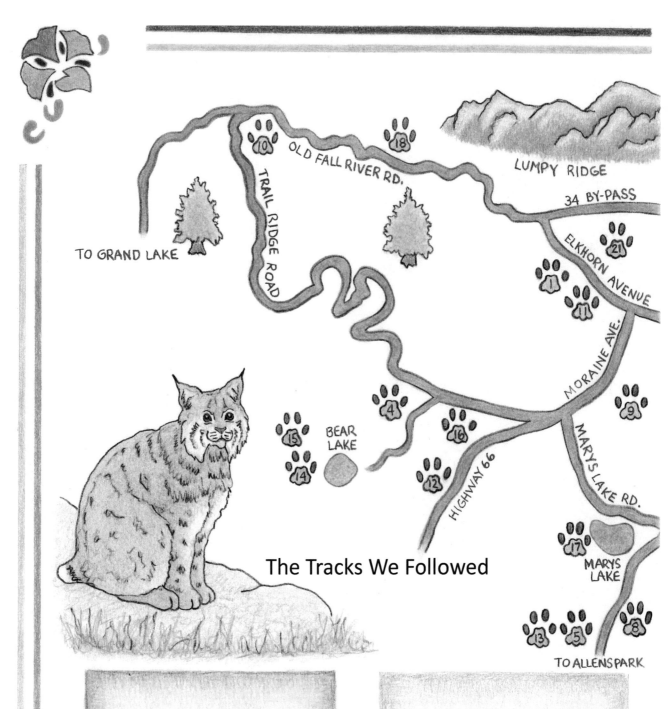

The Tracks We Followed

1) Old Man Mountain
2) Joel Estes and Griff Evans
3) Estes Park Hotel
4) Sprague's Lodge
5) Isabella Bird and
   Rocky Mountain Jim

6) The Stanley Hotel
7) MacGregor Ranch
8) The Enos Mills Cabin
9) Joe Mills' Crags Hotel
10) Trail Ridge Road
11) Elkhorn Lodge

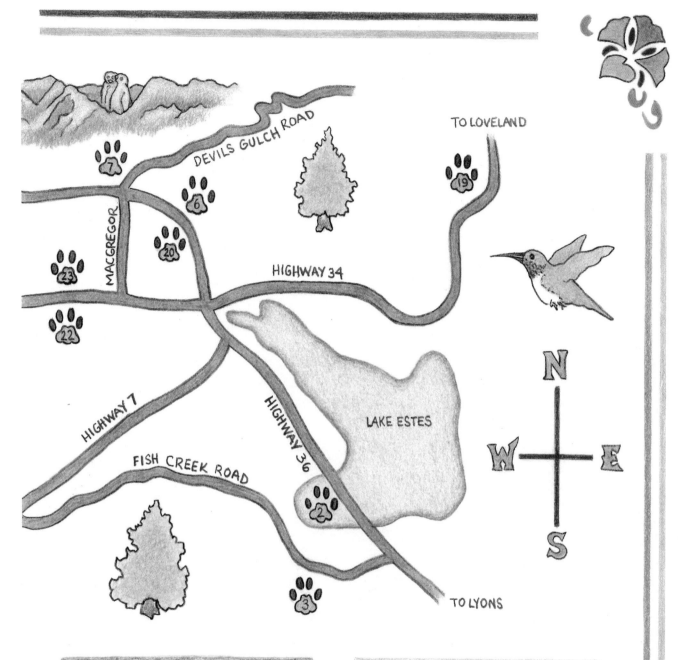

12) YMCA of the Rockies
13) Agnes Vaille Memorial
14) James Patrick
15) Rev. Thornton Sampson
16) Jeff Christiensen Memorial
17) Colorado-Big Thompson Site

18) Lawn Lake Flood
19) Big Thompson Flood
20) Birch Ruins
21) Lewiston Hotel Fire
22) Park Theatre Mall Fire
23) Elkhorn Avenue Parade Route

Glossary

accommodate: provide something needed, such as food or lodging

ascent: climb, the act of rising, the act of climbing a mountain

conduit pipes: a natural or artificial channel through which water flows

conservationist: a person who advocates the careful management or preservation of natural resources

demolish: to tear down, to break to pieces, smash, destroy

encounter: to come upon face to face

establish: to bring into existence

expedition: a journey undertaken for a specific purpose

floor joists: small beams arranged parallel from wall to wall to support a floor

fracture: break, rupture

fraud: intentional trickery, deceit

geologist: a scientist who deals with the history of the earth as recorded in rocks

homestead: public land acquired from the government by filing a record and cultivating the land

incorporation: unite into one body, form into a legal unit

initiate: to cause the beginning of something

legislation: laws and rules that have the force of authority

maim: mutilate, disfigure or wound severely

mangle: injure so severely as to cause lasting damage

memorial: something that keeps memory alive

natural resources: things supplied by nature, such as mineral deposits and water

naturalist: a person who studies and explains the ways of nature

ricochet: to bounce off one object and hit another

ridgeline: a line marking or following the crest or tops of hills or mountains

self-reliant: being dependent on oneself

surveyor: one who measures and records the areas on the earth's surface

tourist: a person who takes a trip and visits places for pleasure

tragedy: a disastrous event, a calamity

Photograph Sources

Contributor Bios

PATRICIA PATERSON PICKERING

Patricia Paterson Pickering grew up in New York and is now a resident of Estes Park and a volunteer at the Estes Park Museum. She graduated from Northwestern University, receiving a Bachelor of Science degree in Education. She has spent her entire professional life in education, with an emphasis on early elementary classes. She taught in schools in Illinois, Michigan and Texas. She has always been fascinated with history, and this book has given her an opportunity to combine her professional skills with one of her major interests.

PATRICIA YEAGER WASHBURN

Patricia Yeager Washburn grew up as a Park Service kid, raised in California and national parks since her father, Dorr Yeager, was a ranger. She attended Reed College and Colorado College, majoring in history. After her marriage and raising four children, she attended Iliff School of Theology. Her ministry included running an inner-city retreat house, teaching in two seminaries and now, semi-retired, serving as chaplain at Good Samaritan Village in Estes Park. She has deep roots in Estes Park, since her grandfather was Joe Mills, Enos Mills' younger brother, and her mother was raised at Crags Lodge. She is incoming Chair of the Board of the Friends & Foundation Inc. of the Estes Park Museum.

PATRICIA HENRIKSEN GREENBERG

Patricia Henriksen Greenberg grew up in New York and received her Bachelor of Fine Arts degree from SUNY Stony Brook. She relocated to Estes Park in 2004, where she continues to find creative expression in the natural world. Patricia has written and illustrated two hand-bound, limited-edition books, *Feather* and *Passing Time Along the Gem Lake Trail*. Most recently she has illustrated the children's picture book, *The Mutt and the Mustang*, by Judy Archibald. She is currently studying Botanical Illustration at the Denver Botanic Gardens.

14218699R00019

Made in the USA
Charleston, SC
28 August 2012